THE LI… OOK OF
CHC…
TIP…

LINDA COLLISTER

THE LITTLE BOOK OF CHOCOLATE TIPS

LINDA COLLISTER

A.
Absolute Press

First published in Great Britain in 2010 by
Absolute Press
Scarborough House, 29 James Street West
Bath BA1 2BT, England
Phone 44 (0) 1225 316013 **Fax** 44 (0) 1225 445836
E-mail info@absolutepress.co.uk
Web www.absolutepress.co.uk

A catalogue record of this book is available from the British Library

ISBN 13: 9781904573982

Printed and bound in Malta on behalf of Latitude Press

'Greetings to you, the lucky finder of this golden ticket, from Mr Willy Wonka!'

Charlie and the Chocolate Factory
Roald Dahl

1

You need to **add a sweetener to anything labelled 100% pure chocolate** –

remember the word chocolate has evolved from the Aztec xocolatl – a bitter frothy drink thickened with maize and flavoured with spices – meaning bitter water. The botanical name is Theobroma cacao 'food of the gods'.

2

For the best,

most luxurious hot chocolate

melt 50g per person good dark chocolate in 150ml milk with a teaspoon of sugar. Whisk well as it comes to the boil then pour into a warmedmug. Add a swirl of whipped cream.

3

Add a little warm gentle spice to hot chocolate

by stirring it with a chocolate cinnamon stick. Dip long cinnamon sticks in melted chocolate leaving the top third plain then leave to set on waxed paper.

4

Store chocolate in a cool, dry place

tightly wrapped and well away from pungent or spicy foods. The fridge is not ideal as if the temperature of the chocolate drops below 13°C as beads of moisture will form as it comes back to room temperature.

5

When melting chocolate, make sure it is broken up into even-sized pieces. Chop chocolate on a very clean and dry chopping board with a large sharp knife, or use a processor working in short bursts or the 'pulse' button.

6

Chocolate melts at 30°C –

remember that 'melt-in-the-mouth' ad – but seizes up around 44°C and starts to burn if heated above 100°C. Even the best chefs have problems melting chocolate so take it gently: put the chopped chocolate into a heatproof bowl. Bring a pan with a little water to the boil. Turn off the heat and set the bowl over the steaming water, making sure the water doesn't touch the base and that water doesn't get into the bowl. Leave to melt then stir gently and remove the bowl from the pan.

7

You can also use the microwave to melt chocolate:

make sure it is completely dry inside and use a dry bowl. Consult the manufacturer's handbook and use a low setting. Check the progress every 10 seconds but remember the chocolate will melt in a different way: the centre of each chunk may be molten while the outer layer is still firm.

8

Try a French Christmas treat:

soak 12 large pitted Agen prunes overnight in a few tablespoons of brandy making sure the cavities get their fair share. Next day fill each cavity with a grape-sized piece of marzipan, mould the prune back into shape, spoon over melted dark chocolate to thickly coat then leave to set. Keep cool, eat within 5 days.

9

If your recipe says to add a liquid when melting chocolate (usually coffee, cream, a liqueur or butter and sometimes water)

add the liquid at the start,

putting it into the bowl with chopped chocolate.

10

To make an instant Hot Mocha

simply stir 2 tablespoons of very good drinking chocolate into a mug of coffee. Then just top with a spoonful of whipped cream.

11

Experiment with flavours:

although Columbus discovered the New World and saw cocoa beans, he never tasted them. It was the Spanish conqueror Cortes who saw the beans used as currency by the Aztecs and realised their economic value. Eventually, the Spanish learnt how to love the beverage, adding honey or cane sugar, vanilla or cinnamon or black pepper to the brew.

12

Spanish nuns in Mexico are thought to have come up with the

first recipe for the chocolate bar in the 17th century.

The first chocolate processing factory in America, Bakers, was established in 1755 by Dr James Baker and John Hannan in Massachusetts; Cadbury's was founded in England in the 1850s – take a tour and see chocolate made.

13

For a thick, richly flavoured milkshake

slice a ripe banana into a food blender, pour in 350ml of ice-cold creamy milk and 2 tablespoons of good quality drinking chocolate. Blend until very smooth then add 50g of melted chocolate and blend until frothy. Pour into a couple of chilled glasses – you can add a scoop of ice-cream or a few ice-cubes.

14

To make small chocolate cups

to hold mousse turn a muffin tin upside down and cover the underside with clingfilm, pressing it down tightly. Pipe swirls of melted chocolate around the sides of each mould to resemble heavy lace with a solid chocolate base.
Pipe a circle of chocolate around each top edge to make a rim to hold the whole cup in place. When set gently lift off the cups.

15

Give robust game or venison dishes a glossy, dark and richly flavoured sauce

by stirring a few squares of dark chocolate into the sauce or gravy at the very end just before serving. Season with plenty of black pepper and a pinch of dried chilli flakes.

16

Try frozen bananas with your ice-cream:

cut off the stalk end, but don't peel. Push a bamboo skewer a quarter way up into each banana. Peel then freeze the bananas overnight on tray lined with wax paper. Melt dark or white chocolate gently in a shallow heatproof dish with a knob of butter. Quickly rotate the bananas in the melted chocolate then eat.

17

Have a chocolate tasting to compare the flavours from different countries. The cocoa tree grows in a narrow band within 10 to 20 degrees of the equator: it needs very high humidity, plenty of rainfall and a constant temperature: try ones from Mexico, Venezuela, Colombia, Brazil, Equador, Ghana, Java, Sri Lanka.

18

Each cocoa tree produces just 3 to 4kg of dried beans each year,

enough for just 3 bars of good chocolate and is very labour-intensive. These dried beans start as shiny seeds inside large rugby-ball shaped pods which grow straight from the tree trunk. They are surrounded by the white shiny flesh of the seed pod and are left to ferment in the sun for several days to develop their unique taste. The beans are then dried, a tricky business given the climate.

19

The classic French chocolate mousse is simple:

melt 100g good dark chocolate with 25g butter and a little brandy. Remove from the heat, leave for a couple of minutes then gently stir in 4 egg yolks (at room temperature). Fold in the stiffly whisked whites. Spoon the mousse into brandy glasses, cover and chill for a couple of hours. Serves 4 to 6.

20

Decorate a special cake or dessert with

fruit dipped in melted dark or white chocolate.

Choose firm dry fruit – strawberries, cherries, cape gooseberries, or glace fruit like pineapple slices or cubes of ginger. Quickly dip, then leave to set on waxed paper in a cool spot – but not the fridge. Use the same day.

21

To make a very dark chocolate sauce put 100g of good dark chocolate, chopped, 100ml of water and 50g of diced butter into a double pan or a heatproof bowl and set over a pan of steaming water. Stir gently until melted and very smooth.

22

Avoid

chocolate made with

artificial vanilla or fats

other than cocoa butter or cocoa fat; 60 to 70% cocoa solids should be perfect. Too high a proportion and the bar can be dry and overwhelming rather than an indication of quality. The chocolate should be balanced – it shouldn't leave your mouth feeling greasy or astringent, or have a harsh or burnt aftertaste.

23

If you're in Brazil you can **try a wonderful milkshake** made from the fresh white flesh from the cocoa pods – the flavour is amazing.

24

Pay for quality.

It is said that white chocolate is the nearest thing to mother's milk, but many people claim that it is not really chocolate, made as it is from cocoa butter (the natural vegetable fat squeezed from the cocoa beans), milk, sugar and vanilla but no cocoa solids.

25

Milk chocolate contains milk (usually condensed), plus flavourings, plenty of sugar and often salt.

Both **milk and plain** chocolate **melt at a** slightly **lower temperature than dark** and burn more easily. For the best flavour choose a brand known for good dark chocolate.

26

White chocolate sauce is very good with fruit,

especially berries, and roast peaches or plums. Break up and gently melt 200g of very good white chocolate then remove from the heat and gradually stir in 200ml of double cream gently heated with 50ml of milk.

27

Decorate cakes with shards of ‘bark’.

Line a baking tray with non-stick paper then spread with melted chocolate about 2mm thick. Leave to set then break into shards. For marbled bark spread melted white or milk chocolate over dark chocolate as it is beginning to set, then quickly marble the two colours with the end of a teaspoon.

28

If you need to grate chocolate

in warm weather chill it for a few minutes before you start then hold the very end with a piece of foil and use the large hole side of the grater.

29

The milky hot chocolate drink

as we know it was invented by a royal doctor – Hans Sloane – as a pick-me-up for Queen Anne's sickly children. He sold his recipe to the Quakers who saw hot chocolate as a healthy alternative to alcohol. Now we know it contains phosphorous, iron, calcium and theobromine which affects the central nervous system and

acts as an anti-depressant

so drink it and feel better!

30

Almond bark is an impressive cake decoration:

you will need equal quantities of chocolate and nuts. Melt the chocolate, and lightly toast the almonds – they can be left whole, bought sliced or cut into 2 or 3 slivers. Mix in the nuts then spread evenly in a fairly thin layer on to a baking tray lined with wax paper. When set break into shards.

31

Cocoa powder

was developed by C.J. van Houten in 1828 when he discovered a way of pressing the cocoa butter from the chocolate then using an alkali to neutralise the excess acid in the powder. It

adds a very powerful but bitter chocolate 'kick'

when dusted onto mousses and cakes.

32

Don't worry **if a white bloom appears on the surface**

of your chocolate. It only means that it has been kept in varying temperatures.

You can still eat it!

33

Seizing happens

when melted chocolate is overheated or it is splashed by a little water, and it then becomes a tight mess rather than a fluid.

It can sometimes be saved:

remove the bowl from the heat and stir in a teaspoon of vegetable oil.

34

If you are making a mousse or mixture that involves

whipped cream

and/or **whipped egg whites, don't overbeat them**

– whip until soft peaks appear (that is the peaks just flop over at the peak rather than standing in stiff peaks). That way they can easily be folded into the chocolate without over-mixing.

35

Leftover chocolate sauces can be covered and stored in the fridge. Reheat gently by standing the pan in another, larger, pan of very hot water.

36

Make a large chocolate bowl

to hold mousse: line a glass or china bowl with clingfilm, leaving the ends hanging over the edge. Paint with at least 4 good layers of melted chocolate, leaving the chocolate to set between each layer. When hard then lift out the clingfilm and chocolate. Peel away the clingfilm then fill.

37

To make curly chocolate ‘wood shavings’

peel a bar of chocolate with a vegetable peeler. This works best at room temperature. To get curved shavings set the bar down in a lined tin, hold it firmly with a sheet of kitchen paper towel then scrape with a melon-ball cutter.

38

Plan to **make chocolate cakes a day before** you want to cut them as the **flavours will develop** and expand overnight, giving a richer taste. They will usually be easier to slice as well.

39

For a special fruit cake replace the usual bag of dried mixed vine fruits with one that's a luxury mix, containing glace cherries and pineapple along with the raisins, currants, sultanas and peel. Roughly chop up a bar of really good dark chocolate and stir in with the dried fruit mixture.

40

Make a rich chocolate fudge icing

for cakes by melting 100g of chopped dark chocolate with a tablespoon of golden syrup and 25g of diced butter in a bowl over a pan of steaming water. Stir frequently until smooth. Leave to cool, stirring occasionally until thick enough to spread.

41

Chocolate shortbread

is a real treat. Cream 200g of soft butter with 100g of caster sugar, then mix in 260g of plain flour and 40g of cocoa powder. Press the mixture into a greased 23cm cake tin, prick well and bake in an oven heated to 180°C/340°F/ Gas 4 for about 15 minutes. Sprinkle with sugar and cut into sections. Remove from the tin when cold.

42

You will need tempered chocolate to

make shiny chocolate eggs or handmade chocolates.

Tempering means to melt and cool chocolate to make it shiny smooth and even in colour. You can use any good chocolate but you will need a candy thermometer.

43

To temper:

melt the chocolate as usual then raise the temperature of the steaming water so the chocolate reaches 45–48°C/113–118°F, stirring gently. Immediately remove the bowl and set in a larger bowl of cool water. Stir until the temperature falls to 27°C/60°C. Replace the bowl over the steaming water and reheat to 29–3°0C/84–86°F.

44

The classic

recipe for truffles

just needs 300g of good dark chocolate, 200ml of cream and cocoa. Put the chopped chocolate into a heatproof bowl, pour over the hot cream and leave for 4 minutes. Stir until smooth then leave until cool. Beat until thick, then roll into marble-sized balls. Chill then quickly dip in melted chocolate. When almost set roll in plenty of cocoa. Cover and chill until needed.

45

To make chocolate 'waves'

spread melted chocolate onto strips of waxed paper then drape the paper up and down over a line of rolling pins, tin cans or glass jars spaced slightly apart. When set, peel the chocolate off the paper in long strips or shorter waves; great for the top of a cake or mousse.

46

Turn your kitchen into an ice cream parlour by making your own chocolate cones. Paint the inside of good quality waffle ice-cream cones with melted chocolate using a pastry brush. Use as soon as the chocolate is set.

47

Brazil nut crunch is another easy treat:

melt 300g of dark chocolate. Pour half into a 20cm cake tin lined with wax paper. Scatter over 100g of roughly chopped brazil nuts and 50g of raisins. Pour over the rest of the chocolate. When set turn out onto a board and chop into pieces with a strong knife.

48

Never try to melt chocolate in a pan set straight onto the top of the stove, or by putting in the oven.

49

Don't store bars of chocolate in the freezer

– it's fine for cakes and cookies as long as they are well wrapped and not left for more than a couple of months.

50

For chocolate fairy buns

beat together 175g of soft butter, 175g of caster sugar, 3 large eggs, a teaspoon of vanilla, 150g of self-raising flour, 30 of cocoa powder and 2 tablespoons of milk. Spoon into 24 paper bun cases set into bun tins and bake in a preheated oven at 180°C/350°F/ Gas 4 for 12–15 minutes until springy. When cold top with fudge icing.

Linda Collister

Linda Collister trained at two world-famous cookery schools – the Cordon Bleu in London and La Varenne in Paris. She went on to become a professional cook, spending several years working for the late Queen Mother, before becoming a food writer. Her great renown is as a baking and chocolate expert. She has written more than 25 food books which have sold all over the world, including *Divine: Heavenly Chocolate Recipes with a Heart* (also for Absolute Press). She is colloquially referred to as the 'Queen of Chocolate'.

THE LITTLE BOOK OF
BARBECUE
TIPS
ANDREW LANGLEY

THE LITTLE BOOK OF
BEER
TIPS
ANDREW LANGLEY

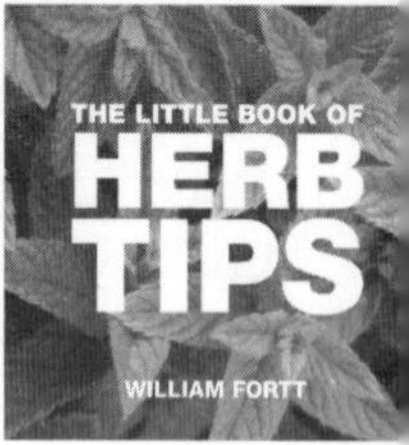
THE LITTLE BOOK OF
HERB
TIPS
WILLIAM FORTT

THE LITTLE BOOK OF
POKER
TIPS
PETER FRENCH

THE LITTLE BOOK OF
GARDENING
TIPS
WILLIAM FORTT

THE LITTLE BOOK OF
CHEFS'
TIPS
RICHARD

THE LITTLE BOOK OF
SPICE
TIPS
ANDREW LANGLEY

THE LITTLE BOOK OF
GOLF
TIPS
PETER FRENCH

THE LITTLE BOOK OF
TIPS
SERIES

THE LITTLE BOOK OF
CHEESE
TIPS
ANDREW LANGLEY

THE LITTLE BOOK OF
WINE
TIPS
ANDREW LANGLEY

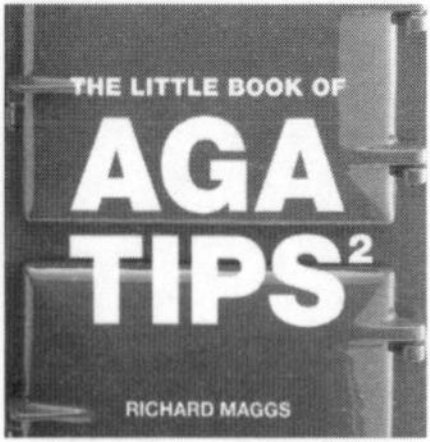
THE LITTLE BOOK OF
AGA
TIPS 2
RICHARD MAGGS

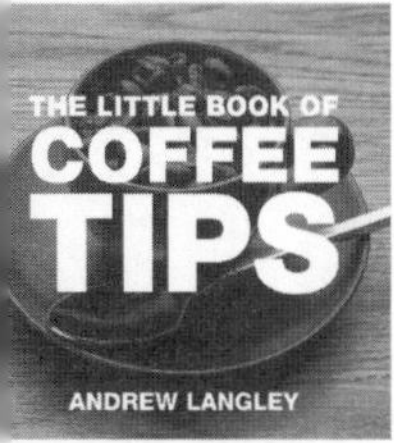
THE LITTLE BOOK OF
COFFEE
TIPS
ANDREW LANGLEY

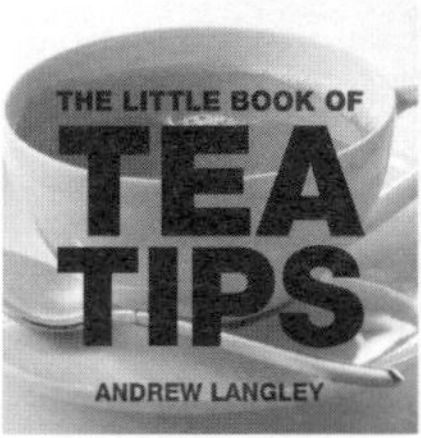
THE LITTLE BOOK OF
TEA
TIPS
ANDREW LANGLEY

THE LITTLE BOOK OF
AGA
TIPS 3
RICHARD MAGGS

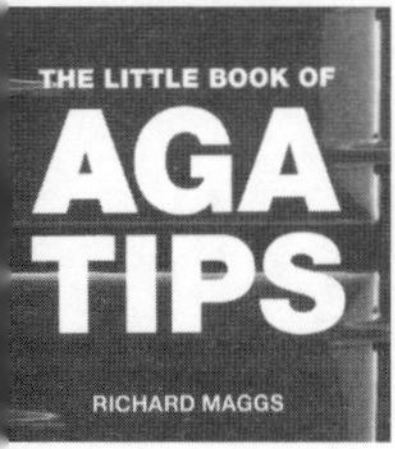
THE LITTLE BOOK OF
AGA
TIPS
RICHARD MAGGS

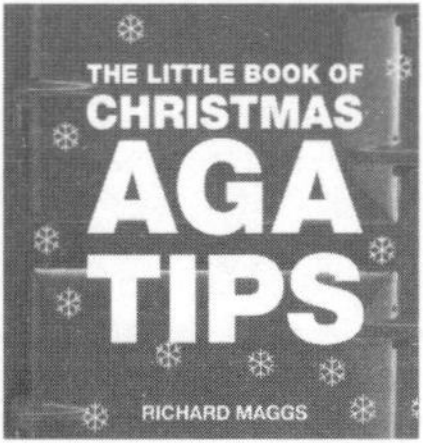
THE LITTLE BOOK OF
CHRISTMAS
AGA
TIPS
RICHARD MAGGS

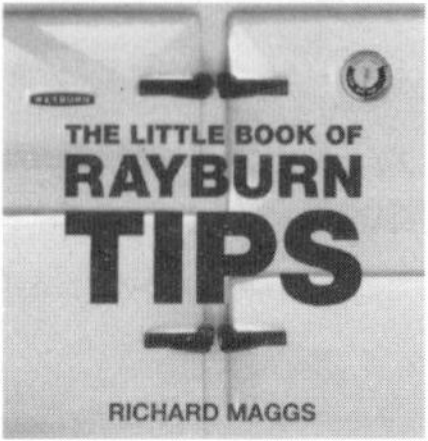
THE LITTLE BOOK OF
RAYBURN
TIPS
RICHARD MAGGS

THE LITTLE BOOK OF
BRIDGE
TIPS
PETER FRENCH

THE LITTLE BOOK OF
CHESS
TIPS
PETER FRENCH

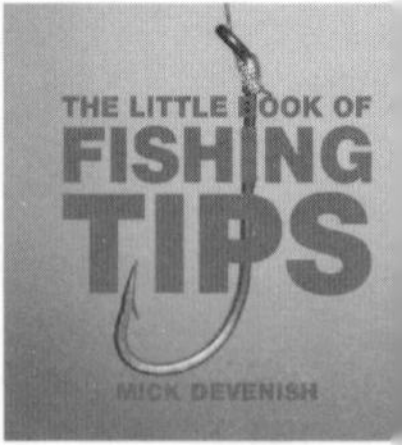
THE LITTLE BOOK OF
FISHING
TIPS
MICK DEVENISH

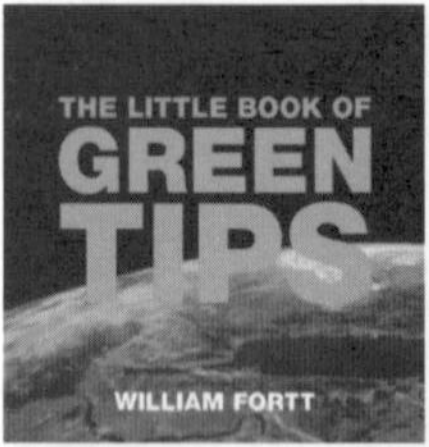
THE LITTLE BOOK OF
GREEN
TIPS
WILLIAM FORTT

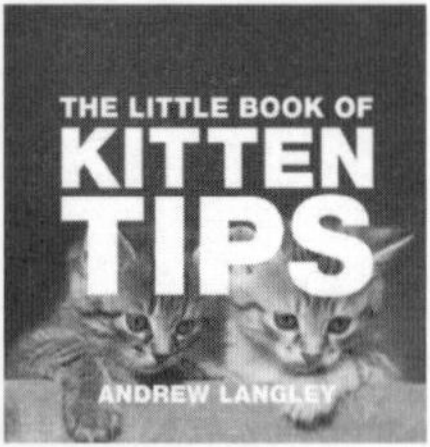
THE LITTLE BOOK OF
KITTEN
TIPS
ANDREW LANGLEY

MARMITE
PAUL HARTLEY
THE LITTLE BOOK OF
MARMITE
TIPS

THE LITTLE BOOK OF
PUPPY
TIPS
ANDREW LANGLEY

THE LITTLE BOOK OF
WHISKY
TIPS
ANDREW LANGLEY

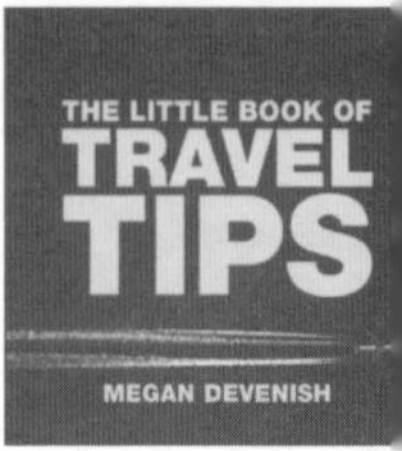
THE LITTLE BOOK OF
TRAVEL
TIPS
MEGAN DEVENISH

Little Books of Tips from Absolute Press

Aga Tips
Aga Tips 2
Aga Tips 3
Christmas Aga Tips
Rayburn Tips
Tea Tips
Coffee Tips
Wine Tips
Whisky Tips
Beer Tips
Cocktail Tips
Cheese Tips
Bread Tips
Herb Tips
Spice Tips
Curry Tips
Marmite Tips
Olive Oil Tips
Vinegar Tips
Pasta Tips
Cupcake Tips
Cake Decorating Tips
Macaroon Tips
Chocolate Tips
Ice Cream Tips
Chefs' Tips
Barbecue Tips
Gardening Tips
Houseplant Tips
Golf Tips
Travel Tips
Fishing Tips
Green Tips
Frugal Tips
Poker Tips
Bridge Tips
Chess Tips
Backgammon Tips
Scrabble Tips
Puppy Tips
Kitten Tips